Daily Affirmations for Weight Loss

Encouragement for those who would want to lose weight and/or to maintain their weight loss goals

TABLE OF CONTENTS

INTRODUCTION

"Arrgh! I've grown so fat! This dress doesn't fit."

"I am just too fat. It will be practically impossible to lose this weight."

"Will he or she want to go out with me, just look at my belly rolls."

These are the thoughts of many obese people. Being overweight/obese is a great concern for society. It can affect an individual's health physically, mentally, emotionally, and sometimes socially. Many overweight people need constant reassurance when it comes to shedding a few pounds.

Every overweight person wishes to lose weight and regain their fitness. However, the majority of these endeavors fail due to a lack of appropriate motivation to continue on track. Affirmations for weight loss are the solution to these troubles.

Daily Affirmations for Weight Loss can be of great benefit. It generally improves one's state of mind and general thinking which will improve the overall quality of living.

CHAPTER ONE

WHAT ARE WEIGHT LOSS AFFIRMATIONS?

Weight loss affirmations can assist you to get rid of your doubts and give you reassurance and strength. It is the act of developing a positive mindset and attitude that will assist in helping you achieve your weight loss goals. It is what you believe that determines your reality. You will act in accordance with your belief and easily overcome obstacles if you believe you can.

Your weight loss objectives will be impracticable and difficult to reach if you believe they are. Anything is possible if you feel you can do anything and that you are on a journey of self-discovery and growth in which anything is conceivable. It all boils down to your self-confidence. When you believe in yourself, you'll be able to push through any difficulties or temptations that come your way.

Positive Affirmations will definitely set you on the right track. Mental health is worsened when one has a poor self-image and being overweight can contribute to it. A negative mindset makes problems seem much bigger than it looks and that is why having a positive attitude when losing weight is extremely important.

Weight loss affirmations make this attitude shift simple. When you practice these weight loss positive affirmations on a daily basis, your thoughts and feelings will gradually shift in the right way, motivating you to take positive action.

CHAPTER TWO

HOW WEIGHT LOSS AFFIRMATIONS HELP

Before you embark on your weight-loss journey, you must first comprehend why you gained weight in the first place and how you may lose it. The majority of people believe they are overweight as a result of overeating and a lack of exercise. This is just partially correct. Overeating and a lack of exercise do, in fact, lead to weight gain. But why did you eat so much to begin with?

A negative emotional state is closely linked to overeating. Comfort foods are a natural shelter when you're experiencing unpleasant feelings like stress, fear, depression, sadness, or insecurity. You eat more sweet and fatty foods when you're anxious or unhappy than you would otherwise.

Positive weight loss affirmations might help you shed the excess weight. Before you consider embarking on a diet or attending a gym, you must first alter your mental state. Replace your pessimism with a healthy dose of optimism and self-assurance. Your mindset should shift from "I am useless" to "Yes, I can do it." Affirmations can aid in this situation.

CHAPTER THREE

HOW TO USE THESE POSITIVE AFFIRMATIONS

Identify the bad ideas you want to get rid of or the manifestation you want to make. Affirmations can be used in both situations, but you must be specific about what you want.

Use the list below as a source of inspiration and direction. Any affirmation can be used as is or modified to make it your own. The most important thing to remember is that the affirmations must connect with you and be statements that you actually believe in.

Choose at least two affirmations and begin utilizing them right away. Begin a daily pattern of reciting the affirmations at least twice a day, for a total of 5-10 minutes per session. Each one should be done at least 10 times each day. Please be patient! Results normally take around a month to appear.

CHAPTER FOUR

POSITIVE AFFIRMATIONS FOR YOUR WEIGHT LOSS JOURNEY

✓ *I have a sound brain and a strong physique that is capable of shedding weight.*

We often complain that it is extremely difficult to lose weight because of one reason or the other. "Oh...I am too busy. I don't have time" or "It is because of my hormonal imbalance?" and so on.

These are all excuses and the worst part is that your brain will believe these excuses. Your body and brain are very powerful. State positive affirmations such as I have a strong body and with hard work and dedication, I am capable of losing weight and the weight loss will follow gradually.

✓ *Today is a great day to achieve my objectives.*

Start your strategy now, rather than waiting until New Year's Day, your birthday, or a major event. Today is a wonderful day to begin repeating your weight-loss affirmations.

- ✓ *I'm not going to wallow in the past. I move forward with enthusiasm, vigor, and purpose.*

  Looking back can be just as demoralizing as looking forward. You've tried so many things before that it's pointless to try again since you'll only be discouraged.

- ✓ *Food can't fill gaps in your heart.*

  An empty heart can only be filled by love. You don't want to miss this opportunity. There are various sorts of hunger. Food, on the other hand, can never satisfy our thirst for love, connection, and companionship. Only love has the power to fill an empty heart.

- ✓ *I am content with my body, heart, and spirit.*

  I am enough. I am whole. As I work towards reducing my weight and improving my health, I am at peace with my body, spirit, and heart.

- ✓ *This is a journey, and I'm going to take each day as it comes.*

  If you have a lot of weight to lose, it can be disheartening and impossible to lose the weight—so just take it one day at a time. Don't get ahead of yourself in your imagination or give up before you even start. Just concentrate on now.

✓ *I don't eat my feelings; I feel them.*

Emotional eating can be very dangerous. This is because this is one of the easiest ways to pack extra unwanted pounds. Cookies or chips and pizza may provide a momentary "hit of bliss," however, REAL SATISFACTION comes from accomplishing your weight loss objectives and taking responsibility for your decisions.

✓ *My body and mind are both healing.*

As I embark on this weight loss journey, putting in my best and staying positive in my thinking, my mind and body are healing and getting much better.

✓ *It is simple for me to stick to a healthy food plan.*

I am thrilled to start a meal plan that is good for my health and will help me have a healthy weight.

✓ *Every day, I make better choices.*

I am proud of myself for taking the bold step of starting this weight loss journey. Every day I am making better eating choices, sleeping habits, and drinking lots of water which will be beneficial to my health.

✓ *I'm not going to compare myself to others. I'm on my own path.*

It's possible that you started your weight reduction journey alongside someone else and they've made more progress than you have. It's critical that you don't compare yourself to others. More exercise, stricter dietary choices, more sleep, less stress, and possibly a more optimistic outlook than you, are among the causes of the difference. Simply work at your own pace and you will lose weight in due time.

✓ *I am a weight loss success story.*

Start picturing yourself as a healthier, skinner version of yourself six months from now. Think of how light you would feel, how your clothes fit on nicely and how proud you would be of yourself for coming this far. Having this winning mentality can undoubtedly aid your weight loss journey.

✓ *I love myself.*

This is a positive affirmation that one should have generally, not just for weight loss. However, it is extremely an important factor that will make your weight loss journey more eventful. You love yourself, and you forgive yourself if you cheat on occasion or if you miss your workout. Remember…it is a journey, not a race…so be kind to yourself!

✓ *I am not controlled by food.*

So frequently, our food choices feel like they're in charge of us, and we're left to our whims. You have the option of eating food that is beneficial to your health. You control what you eat not the other way around.

✓ *I exercise and immediately see an increase in my energy, stamina, and strength.*

I notice how my energy, stamina, and strength increase as I am working out and I want to continue to feel this way. This feeling always helps boost my mood.

✓ *I'll keep trying till I succeed.*

The important thing is to keep trying to move forward. It's fine if some days are better than others. Simply make a commitment for today and keep going hour after hour. If things get very terrible, keep repeating this weight loss affirmation every half hour.

✓ *Every day, I'm getting better.*

This is one of the weight-loss affirmations that emphasizes minor victories. Every day, even on the days when you miss your mark, you improve.

As a result, celebrate tiny victories like:

Instead of four cookies, I ate two.

I didn't go to the gym but I walked for 15 minutes

Instead of chips, I'm having a little salad for lunch.

✓ *My Curves and Thickness are Embraced*

If you're a full-figured or plus-sized lady, this is one of the most crucial weight-loss affirmations. So, while you commit to your weight loss quest, love your curves and thickness as this is a beautiful trait to have.

✓ *I'm not ashamed of my appearance.*

Being self-conscious about your appearance can lead to depression and other mental and emotional problems. Shame puts in motion a vicious cycle that leads to overeating, weight gain, and more shame.

This is a vital affirmation for weight loss since it helps you break the cycle of shame. Don't go along with the naysayers.

"It is what it is," say to yourself in the mirror. This is who I am, and I am not ashamed of my appearance."

✓ *I'm dedicated to achieving my objectives.*

Because you must be devoted to reducing weight and keeping it off, this is one of the most vital affirmations for weight reduction. It's crucial to be explicit about your weight loss goal if you want to stick to it. Goals are different from desires. As a result, you must write down your goals and read them every day.

✓ *I enjoy the feeling I get after working out*

Working out helps to reduce stress and depression and creates a general happy feeling. Always look forward to exercising because of the amazing feeling after.

✓ *It's easier to lose weight now that I have a positive attitude*

Positive thinking leads to positive results, and the same is true for weight loss. Weight loss appears to be easier to achieve when you have a good attitude.

✓ *I believe in myself and acknowledge my greatness.*

I can do this, slow and steady wins the race. Consistency is key and I am trying. The weight will come off.

✓ *I am not defined by the number on the scale.*

This is so true. I am making progress even if the scale doesn't change. The body feels lighter, clothes feel looser!

✓ *I let go of the stress and tension that comes with reducing weight quickly.*

I will take this process slowly. I didn't add this weight in one day and I will not lose it in a day either. I will go through this weight loss process gradually and continually.

✓ *I am becoming a better version of myself every day.*

I am improving and getting stronger and better at achieving my weight loss goals.

✓ *I am tenacious and dedicated.*

I am fully committed to this weight loss journey and I will strive, stay focused and be determined to get to my desired weight.

✓ *I am happy with my progress so far.*

Even if I lose 1 pound of fat, I am proud of this achievement. One day 1 pound will be 25 pounds down!

✓ *My eating habits are in line with my ultimate goal of decreasing weight.*

My food choices will help me lose the weight and therefore I am making the right decision and I will stick to my meal plan to achieve desired weight loss.

✓ *I drink sufficient water to keep my body going.*

I know that eating the right foods and drinking enough water will help my body's metabolism and therefore accelerate weight loss.

✓ *I am capable of achieving anything I set my mind to.*

I will succeed at any of my desired goals and this also includes losing weight. I will set my mind up for success and weight loss will follow.

✔ *My body needs nutritious meals and regular exercise.*

I am eating healthy foods that my body needs and in addition to this, I am also losing weight. I am also exercising to keep fit, stay alert, and active and my body needs this as well.

✔ *My health is my number one priority.*

Health is Wealth. I will stay focused on my weight loss goal because it won't only help improve my appearance but also, my health will also improve.

✔ *I am not addicted to junk food.*

I eat healthy now and I can cope without eating junk foods. Junk foods impede my weight loss and I can stop eating them as they are not helpful for my health or weight.

✔ *I envision my dream body and take action to make it a reality.*

Every day, I will remind myself of why I started this journey. I want to achieve a dream body and I will do my very best and not give up, until I achieve it. If many people have achieved this, so can I.

✓ *Every time I overcome temptation, I improve my self-control.*

I know I have to be very disciplined if I want to achieve my weight loss goal. I am proud each and every time I overcome temptation because this means I am getting stronger and my self-control is improving.

✓ *I'm finding new foods that are both delicious and good for me.*

I have realized that healthy foods can be delicious too and they are quite nutritious and healthy for my body. This will make weight loss easier and resist the temptation for eating unhealthy foods.

✓ *It makes me happy to know that my hard work is paying off.*

I feel lighter and I'm happier. My hard work is not in vain and I feel amazing!

✓ *My dishes are always prepared with the best ingredients available.*

I use healthy ingredients that are nutritious to my body to prepare my meals. My body is getting the required nutrients that it needs.

✓ *I deserve a healthy body.*

I will eat healthy foods as this will improve my psyche, mentally, physically, emotionally, and socially. I will feel happier and more confident and I won't be easily prone to diseases.

✓ *I accept my body, flaws and all, and am content with it while working on my new body.*

I am a wonderful person and my body is mine. Even though my body is not yet the way I want it to look, I still accept it with its flaws because it is the machine that enables me to carry out daily tasks. It is this body I have now that will help me attain the body I'm aspiring to have.

✓ *I'm proud of myself for making the decision to live a healthy lifestyle.*

Heck yeah! I am really pleased with myself for choosing to have a healthier lifestyle in the first place. I am proud of myself for taking this bold step and I will embrace the whole process.

✓ *I am confident that I will be able to achieve my weight loss goals.*

I am doing all that will help me lose weight and I will certainly lose this weight!

✓ *My body is becoming smaller every single day.*

Even though I may not notice, I am reducing every day and I am one step closer to my goal weight every day that passes.

✓ *I treat myself with kindness and respect.*

I will be kind to myself. I may slip up sometimes, but I will get right back on track. A moment of weakness when I go off my diet will not distort weeks of progress.

✓ *I am becoming a weight loss success inspiration for many people.*

When I reach my goal weight, I will inspire a lot of people and I will encourage them that weight loss is possible. I may be losing weight for myself but I am also helping others to lose weight as well.

✓ *I am pleased by how much energy and vitality I have.*

Eating healthy and exercising regularly generally boosts energy levels and vitality. This makes me feel great while I still continue to lose weight.

✓ *Snacking and eating in between meals is not beneficial to me or my weight loss goals.*

I need to be fully committed to this weight loss process. Snacking slows down my progress and makes the process take longer than it should. Therefore, I will desist from it.

CHAPTER FIVE

MORE WONDERFUL AFFIRMATIONS

✓ *My body is a temple for me. I make sure to only put beneficial things in the machine that will keep it functioning properly and help me achieve my weight reduction objectives.*

These things include positive attitudes, eating healthy, and exercising regularly. These are all the necessary things I need that will help my body run smoothly and help me achieve my weight loss goals effectively.

✓ *I lose weight one pound at a time.*

I am not going to expect to lose a lot of weight in a single moment. I will lose the weight gradually. If I lose the weight too quickly, I may put it on back quickly again. Gradual weight loss is massive progress.

✓ *My desire to be slimmer outweighs my cravings.*

This affirmation helps when the cravings hit. I will remember how far I have come and how yielding to this craving may affect my progress. I want to be slimmer and this is more important than any craving I may have.

✓ *Exercising is now a part of my daily routine.*

Exercising is good for my health, wellness, and fitness and I will make it a part of my daily routine.

✓ *My excess fat is vanishing, revealing my powerful, lean muscles.*

My body and muscles are becoming toned and fit, as the fat is melting away.

✓ *I am a real and living example of someone who is completely committed to their weight loss goal.*

I want to be seen as someone who commits to weight loss goals and achieves them. This will help me stick to my healthy meal choices and my exercise regimen.

✓ *I am mentally and physically competent.*

I have become mentally and physically strong to carry out my weight loss goals. I have started and I am doing the best that I can, and in no time, I will achieve my goals.

✓ *I'm constantly working on adopting healthier eating habits.*

I am working on finding different ways to enjoy healthy eating and trying out different delicious healthy options for weight loss. I will constantly do this to lose the weight efficiently.

✓ *The entire universe is conspiring to assist me in losing weight and fat.*

I believe the universe is also cheering me on in my weight loss journey and as long as I have a positive attitude and do the right thing, the weight loss will naturally follow.

✓ *I am definitely shedding inches.*

The scale may not show a significant difference but I know I am definitely losing inches around my arms, waist, and legs. I make progress every day.

✓ *I'm amazed at how far I've come with my weight loss and how far I've come.*

I started this journey two months ago and I have constantly kept to my regime. I am proud of myself and I have lost 10 pounds. I am in awe and I will continue to press forward.

✓ *I am the best version of myself, and I am constantly striving to improve.*

I am whole and amazing now. I am working hard to improve this version of myself so I can become the best possible version of myself.

✓ I have a weight-loss strategy that I am following.

I have a plan in place to achieve my weight loss goals and I am proud of myself for sticking to it. I feel great knowing that I am trying to do the right thing and getting the benefits for it.

✓ *I recognize myself in ways other than food.*

I find meaning and fulfillment in life in ways that are not linked to food. I am a good person. I help others. I am doing the best I can.

✓ *I'm pumped to go to the gym.*

I will always psyche myself up and be pumped and ready to go to the gym. I will always do this because no matter how little I work out, I'm one step closer to my weight loss goal. Plus, I always feel great after each workout!

✓ *I'm not going to give up on my diet goals, and I'm going to see them through.*

*"I'm a survivor. I'm not going to give up. I will survive, keep on surviving"-**Destiny's Child-Survivor.*** This is my anthem, the end justifies the means, I won't give up until I achieve my desired weight.

✓ *Eating healthy has become as natural to me as breathing.*

I have adopted these healthy eating habits and I have become so used to them that it has become second nature to me. Healthy foods make me skinner and more agile.

✓ *I am losing weight because I want and need it.*

My body needs to be at a normal weight for me to be able to function optimally. I also want to look good and feel good and losing weight is worth the effort.

✓ *My metabolism is great.*

I have a great metabolism and with my proper eating and exercise choices, I'll crush my weight loss goals in no time.

✓ *I let go of any guilt when I mess up about food choices.*

To err is human, to forgive is divine. I am human and I mess up sometimes. I refuse to feel guilty because I went off my diet because of a craving. Instead, I embrace myself for how far I have come and I will simply get back on track again.

✓ *All of my desires come true because I am a success magnet.*

I attract success because I am a hard worker and I believe in myself. My weight loss desires will definitely come true.

✓ *I have the ability to change my life for the better.*

I can change and become a better person as long as I put my mind to it. I will not stop until I achieve the greatest version of the person I can be.

✓ *My reward is the strong, sturdy, and healthy lifestyle I will achieve.*

I am looking forward to my reward of having a healthy and sturdy body. I will also feel happier and skinner when my hard work pays off.

✓ *I'm overjoyed that my clothes are now more comfortable.*

I can notice changes in how my clothes fit my body and I feel ecstatic that my efforts are showing.

✓ *I'm establishing lifelong healthy behaviors.*

My weight loss journey is helping me to become more disciplined and committed. It is ultimately helping to develop good habits that will last throughout my life.

✓ *I naturally seek out information and ideas for effective weight loss by reading and viewing content on weight loss.*

I am dedicated to this weight loss journey and I naturally seek out ideas that will help me achieve successful weight loss.

✓ *I am my own personal cheerleader.*

I will continue to encourage myself to continue to press on in my weight loss journey. I am doing a great job and I am happy with the efforts I have put in.

✓ *I love how I look when I see myself in the mirror.*

When I look in the mirror, I am proud of the reflection I see. I see someone who has decided to take the right path and is trying to do the right thing!

✓ *I constantly engage in energy-generating and fat-burning workouts.*

I am consistently burning fat and increasing my energy levels each day and I feel great each time I do it.

✓ *I only eat when I am hungry.*

I eat only when I absolutely need to. I do this so I won't gain unnecessary pounds.

✓ *I only want to consume healthy delicious foods.*

I only desire to eat foods that are healthy and wholesome for my body and that would greatly help me to achieve my weight loss goals.

✓ *I deserve a slim, fit, and attractive body.*

I deserve to have a slim and attractive body and I am working very hard to achieve this by eating out and working out regularly.

✓ *I am creating a healthy lifestyle for myself.*

This weight loss journey is generally making me healthy even after I reach my weight loss goals and I will always be in great health.

✓ *Every day, I wake up with a clear goal in mind: to reach my target weight.*

Every day is a brand new day and I wake up knowing that I am one step closer to reaching my target weight and I can do this effectively.

✓ *My ideal weight is easy for me to achieve and maintain.*

I can definitely achieve my ideal weight because I am doing my very best and I have confidence in myself to do so.

✓ *I have complete control over how much food I consume.*

I am in full control of what I put into my body. I decide what I eat and what I won't eat. I will eat only foods that will aid my weight loss journey.

✓ *Every physical exercise I make assists me to burn excess fat in my body and maintain my desired body weight.*

I burn excess fat when I move around. Even when I am doing basic chores or walking up the stairs and these little steps also help me to reach my goal weight.

✓ *I look and feel fantastic, and I am pleased with every aspect of my weight-loss efforts.*

I look and feel wonderful. I am happy with the daily changes I make to help improve my body and my mind.

✓ *My appetite for bad meals is dwindling on a regular basis.*

My appetite for unhealthy foods keeps reducing because I am getting familiar with eating healthy meals and I feel great.

✓ *It's simple for me to make minor changes on a daily basis because I have an inner determination that goes beyond food, weight, and the scale.*

Better changes to my eating and exercising habits are getting simpler because I am extremely determined to achieve a healthy body and It goes beyond food, weight, and the numbers on the scale.

✓ *I let go of the desire to judge my body, and I confirm that my weight loss is independent of my previous successes or failures.*

I will not put undue stress on how quickly the pounds come off and I will not compare this weight loss experience to my previous failed attempts or my more successful attempts in the past.

✓ *I am pleased with my hard work and perseverance, and I can sense a significant internal shift in my body and mind that is very positive.*

I am working very hard and I am focused. I am really happy with this and I can sense a positive and rewarding shift in my body and mind.

✓ *My thoughts encourage me to continue on my weight-loss journey.*

I will continue to uplift my spirits and encourage myself throughout my entire weight loss journey. I owe this to myself.

✓ *The thin inner me is bursting forth with excitement.*

I can already foresee and feel the slimmer version of myself and I am beaming with happiness. I am rejoicing that all my hard work has paid off.

✓ *God is assisting and supporting my weight loss journey.*

I trust and believe that God will strengthen me. He will help me in this weight loss journey and I have faith that I would reach my goals with his help.

✓ *I am successfully achieving my weight loss goals.*

I am losing weight and getting closer to my weight loss goals. I am successful at weight loss and I will exceed my expectations!

✓ *I'll keep eating healthy even after I attain my objective.*

I have adopted a healthy lifestyle. I will continue to eat healthy even after I have attained my goal weight so I can keep being healthy.

✓ *I now use positive affirmations to assist me in losing weight.*

I have now recognized the power of positive affirmations. It tremendously helps in my weight loss journey and makes the experience easier and more worthwhile.

CONCLUSION

Losing weight is not an easy task. One needs all the assurance one can get. This list of positive weight loss affirmations will surely help anyone who wants to embark on a weight loss journey. They may seem small but they help significantly with the weight loss process.

One should recite 10 affirmations every day before beginning a diet or an exercise regime. With these affirmations which will strengthen you, and with your weight loss program in place, it is definitely certain that your weight loss goals will be achieved.

REFERENCES

Chasing Vibrance. (2020.) *"15 Positive Affirmations for Weight Loss"*

https://chasingvibrance.com/facts-about-texas/7-weight-loss-affirmations-to-keep-you-motivated/

Abundance No Limits. *"50 Powerful Weight Loss Affirmations"*

https://www.abundancenolimits.com/weight-loss-affirmations/

The Veg Query. *"50 Weight Loss Affirmations"*

https://thevegquery.com/weight-loss-affirmations/

Camp, N. (2016.) *"50 Weight Loss Affirmations".* Committed to Myself. *https://committed to myself.com/50-weight-loss-affirmations/*

Hanson, K. (2021.) *"Inspiring List of 874 Weight Loss Affirmation To Reach Your Goals"*. The Right Affirmations. *https://therightaffirmations.com/weight-loss-affirmations/*

James, D. (2021.) *"13 Daily Affirmations for Weight Loss"*. Keep it Tight Sisters. *https://keepittightsisters.com/13-daily-affirmations-for-weight-loss/*

Kristenson, S. (2021.) *"65 Affirmations To Help With Your Weight Loss Efforts"*. Happier Human. *https://www.happierhuman.com/affirmations-weight-loss/*

Mishra, A. *"50 Best Weight Loss Affirmations To Get Your Perfect Body"*. Awesome AJ. *https://awesomeaj.com/2014/10/28/best-weight-loss-affirmations-perfect-body/*